Not just for Christmas

Roddy Doyle

Roddy Doyle grew up in Dublin and worked as an English and geography teacher before becoming a full-time writer in 1993. His novels include *The Barrytown Trilogy (The Commitments, The Snapper, and The Van)* and *Paddy Clarke, Ha Ha Ha*, which won the 1993 Booker Prize. The film version of *The Commitments* became an international success.

Cornelsen Open Door
© Roddy Doyle, 2002
This edition of *Not just for Christmas* is published by
arrangement with New Island Books Ltd.

Umschlaggestaltung
Ellen Meister
(nach Originalausgabe von *Artmark*, Cork, Irland)

www.cornelsen.de

1. Auflage, 1. Druck 2006

Alle Drucke dieser Auflage sind inhaltlich unverändert und
können im Unterricht nebeneinander verwendet werden.

© 2006 Cornelsen Verlag, Berlin

Das Werk und seine Teile sind urheberrechtlich geschützt.
Jede Nutzung in anderen als den gesetzlich zugelassenen
Fällen bedarf der vorherigen schriftlichen Einwilligung des
Verlages.
Hinweis zu § 52a UrhG: Weder das Werk noch seine Teile
dürfen ohne eine solche Einwilligung eingescannt und in ein
Netzwerk eingestellt werden.
Dies gilt auch für Intranets von Schulen und sonstigen
Bildungseinrichtungen.

Druck: *CPD*, Ebbw Vale, Großbritannien

ISBN-13: 978-3-06-031814-8
ISBN-10:   3-06-031814-X

CHAPTER ONE

Danny Murphy was going to meet his brother.

He wrote in his notebook: "Meeting my brother at 8 o'clock." He knew it looked silly. "My brother" instead of "Jimmy", his brother's name.

When he spoke to Jimmy on the phone, two days ago, Jimmy had called himself "Jim". And their mother still called him James. Jimmy or Jim or James. Danny didn't know what to call him.

He hadn't seen or heard from Jimmy in twenty years. More. Twenty-one years.

But then, two days ago, the phone rang.

"Dad?"

His son, Little Dan, shouted from the hall downstairs.

"Yes?" said Danny.

He was upstairs, shaving.

"Jim wants you," said Little Dan.

Danny wiped his face with a towel as he went down the stairs. He knew a few men called Jim. So he didn't know who he'd be talking to when he picked up the phone.

"Hello?"

"Danny?"

"Yes?"

"It's Jim."

Danny waited for more. He didn't know the voice.

"Jim, your brother."

"Oh."

That was all. "Oh." Danny could think of nothing else to say. No other words came to him.

His brother spoke again.

"How are you?" he asked.

"Fine," said Danny. "Yourself?"

"Grand."

"Good," said Danny.

"So. Do you want to meet?"

"OK," said Danny.

"For a pint or something."

"OK."

And now, here he was. It was two days later and he was on his way to meet Jimmy. His long-lost brother.

The bus was coming up to his parents' house. It was the house he had grown up in.

It was the house Danny and Jimmy Murphy had grown up in.

CHAPTER TWO

They were never apart, the Murphy brothers. Jimmy was a year older than Danny, so they weren't twins. But they were *like* twins. Everybody said it. Their parents, their sisters, the neighbours. They all said it. Even the O'Connor sisters down the road said it, and they were twins.

It wasn't just because they were always together. There was more to it than that. They didn't have to speak to each other. That was it. One brother always knew what the other one wanted or needed. Danny would pass the salt to Jimmy just before Jimmy put his hand out for it. Danny would pass the ball to Jimmy without having to look first.

Once, a teacher was just about to smack Jimmy for not having a red biro. Then there was a knock on the classroom door. And Danny walked in – with a red biro. Most of the boys in the class clapped but one or two started crying.

They were never apart. Through primary school and secondary school, they were always side by side. Games, gangs, football, girls, Guinness – they discovered them all together. They both got Lego from Santa. They both got their first kiss from the same girl. (Mind you, so did every other boy in the parish.) They got drunk together the first time. They shared the same hangover the next morning. They shared their money. They shared their clothes. They shared their lives.

They shared the same bed.

"Go to sleep!" their mother shouted.

The kitchen was under the bedroom. Her voice came through the floor-boards.

This happened when Jimmy was ten and Danny was nine.

They put their heads under the blankets so their mother wouldn't hear them laughing. And they met the smell that had made them laugh in the first place.

Jimmy's farts were famous.

"Oh, God!"

Danny tried to get his head out from under the blanket. But Jimmy wouldn't let him. He held Danny's head down on the mattress. Danny kicked and tried to get away from Jimmy's grip.

He could hear their mother.

"If I have to come up to you, there will be two sorry boys in the Murphy house!"

Danny pushed and pulled but he couldn't move Jimmy. His neck was sore. He couldn't breathe. He had stopped laughing a long time ago. Jimmy's fingers were hurting his neck.

He tried to yell for his mother.

CHAPTER THREE

Danny remembered this as the bus went past his mother's house. He could still smell the mattress. Thirty years after it had happened. More. Thirty-three years. He could still feel Jimmy's fingers on his neck as he pushed his face into the sheet.

There was no light on in the old bedroom, or in any of the front rooms. There was only his mother living in there now. It was Wednesday. She'd be watching *Coronation Street*. She hadn't missed it since 1967. Not once. She took the phone off the hook while it was on. And she ate a Cadbury's Flake very, very slowly. The last little bit of chocolate went into her mouth just as the music came on at the end. Even on the day they buried Danny's father she watched *Coronation Street*.

"He'd have wanted me to watch it," she said.

And they all agreed with her. Danny's father had loved *Coronation Street* as well.

They all watched it with her. Danny, his sisters, Una and Mary, and his mother's sister, Rose.

Una pointed at the ceiling.

"He's up there in Heaven, Mammy, watching it with us."

"Shush," said Danny's mother, "I can't hear."

Jimmy wasn't there. He didn't turn up for the funeral. He sent flowers and a telegram.

"Does he think it's a wedding?" said Rose.

"Shush," said Danny's mother. "He's very busy over there."

"Over there" was London. Jimmy lived in London. He'd been living there for twenty-one years. He came home now and again but Danny never saw him. And Danny had never been to London.

They were meeting in Todd's. It was two bus stops away. Danny looked at his watch. He was a bit early. He didn't want to be there first.

He stood up and rang the bell.

He was going to walk the rest of the way. He'd walk slowly. Very slowly. He'd crawl. There was no way he was going to be there first. Jimmy was going to have to wait for him. For once in his life.

Suddenly, the bus turned left and Danny fell onto a seat. He almost landed on top of an old woman who was sitting beside the window.

"Sorry," he said.

He stood up again.

"Mind yourself, love," said the old woman.

His face was red. He could feel the heat in his cheeks. He walked carefully to the door. "Have a nice day," said the driver, and the bus took off so quickly it nearly took Danny's arse with it.

He pulled his jacket across his chest. It was cold. There were drops of rain in the air but it wasn't really raining yet.

Danny took his time.

He looked at his watch again. If it took him ten minutes to walk to Todd's he'd only be five minutes late. That wasn't enough. Jimmy was going to be five minutes late anyway. At least five. He was always late. At least, he was always late twenty years ago.

Danny knew he wasn't being fair. It was more than twenty years since he'd had to wait for Jimmy. People changed. They were different people now, the two of them. Danny had changed. So, Jimmy had probably changed too.

Still he didn't go any faster. There was

no way he was going to walk into Todd's before Jimmy.

CHAPTER FOUR

"What age are you?" said the barman.

"Twenty-one," said Jimmy, and he looked right back at the barman.

Jimmy was really seventeen.

The barman nodded at Danny.

"And what about your little brother?" he said.

"He's twenty-two," said Jimmy.

Danny nearly fell over. He was only sixteen.

They were in Todd's, the only pub that their father never came into. It was dark, and quiet, and secret, and great. Danny wanted to stay.

The barman looked at Danny. Then he smiled. He knew Jimmy was lying. But Jimmy got away with things like that. If Danny had said it, he'd have been kicked out.

"What will it be?" said the barman.

"Two pints of Guinness," said Jimmy.

Again, Danny nearly fell over. They had agreed on it before they came in, outside on the street. Smithwicks. They were going to drink Smithwicks. Guinness was serious stuff. Too much for first-time drinkers. Guinness had to be handled with care.

"Two pints it is," said the barman. "But come here. Just say 'Two pints' in future. There's no need to say 'of Guinness'. What else would it be in Dublin?"

Danny watched Jimmy's skin go red, from the neck up into his cheeks.

"Ha ha," said Danny when the barman went to pull the pints.

"Ha ha, what?" said Jimmy.

"Two pints," said Danny.

"I'll give you two kicks if you don't shut up," said Jimmy.

The 28th of June. 1973. Saturday. Three minutes past eight o'clock. Danny remembered it perfectly. Their first time in a pub. Todd's. The two of them together. The Murphy brothers.

The barman took his time. They stood at the bar. They cursed the barman. He was taking forever. They wanted to get the pints, so they could go into a corner and hide. Every time the door opened Danny looked to see who was coming in. He was sure it would be their father.

"Stop looking," said Jimmy.

The barman was there again, with the pints.

"Expecting someone, lads?" said the barman.

"No," said Jimmy.

"Your da, maybe?" said the barman.

"He's dead," said Jimmy.

Danny nearly fell over, again.

"Oh dear," said the barman. "That's bad news. He looked fine when I played golf with him on Saturday."

And again, Danny saw Jimmy's face go red. This time Danny spoke.

"Our da doesn't play golf," he said. It was true.

"*Doesn't?*" said the barman. "You said he was dead."

"*Didn't,*" said Danny. "When he wasn't dead. He never played golf."

The barman was joking. Danny saw that now.

"It must be somebody else," said the barman.

"Yes," said Danny.

"Some other man called Murphy," said the barman.

"Yes," said Danny.

"Enjoy your pints," said the barman.

"Thank Jesus," said Danny, to himself.

He grabbed his pint and ran to a table in a corner far away from the barman.

Jimmy got there before him.

"He doesn't play golf, does he?" said Jimmy.

"The barman?"

"No!" said Jimmy. "Da."

"I don't think so," said Danny. "He doesn't have any clubs. And he works on Saturdays. But how did the barman know our name is Murphy?"

"Ah, who cares?" said Jimmy. "Cheers."

He lifted his pint. Danny lifted his. Danny didn't like the smell that was getting closer as he lifted the glass to his mouth. He hoped the taste would be better. He put the glass to his lips. He tried to keep it well away from his nose.

He had never tasted anything like it in his life. It was horrible, disgusting. It was brutal. He had never tasted anything as bad. He was going to be sick. He was sure he was. He wanted to run home.

He put the glass down.

"Lovely," he said.

Jimmy put the glass down.

"Yes," said Jimmy.

Danny looked at Jimmy's glass. He had hardly touched it. It was nearly full, like Danny's.

But after three more pints it was lovely.

They sat side by side and slowly filled their guts with Guinness. They watched the men and women coming and going. And after a while they began to feel at home, in the middle of the smoke and chat.

"I don't like yours," said Jimmy.

He said it every time a woman walked into the bar. By the third pint it was the funniest thing Danny had ever heard in his life. And he said, "I don't like yours" every time a man walked into the bar.

They felt like men. They shared the feeling. They were growing up together. The Murphy brothers.

And Danny *did* get sick.

On the way home.

Outside the chipper.

He opened his mouth and all the Guinness and everything else he had ever drunk or eaten fell out of him, onto the ground.

"Oh Jesus!" he said.

He wiped his eyes. When he looked again, he saw Jimmy getting sick beside him.

CHAPTER FIVE

Danny knew where he had puked that night. Twenty-five years ago. More. Twenty-six years. But he still knew the spot. Beside the post-box, outside the chipper.

He looked at the spot. It was clean. Twenty-six years of rain had washed away Danny's puke. And Jimmy's.

The chipper wasn't a chipper anymore. It was an estate agency. Danny went over to the window. It would kill another few minutes. It was still too early to go into Todd's and meet Jimmy. He looked at the photographs of the houses.

The prices. Jesus Christ. A house like

the one he grew up in was going for £120,000. That was mad money. You could buy a lot of chips with that kind of money.

He knew some of the houses in the window. He knew who had lived in them when he was a kid. The one the Mad Woman had lived in was going for £115,000. They called her the Mad Woman because she never took her coat off and she had no children or husband. Danny wondered was the Mad Woman dead. He had given her that name.

That was Danny's job when they were kids. He made up all the nicknames.

He knew another of the houses for sale in the window. Number 26. Two doors from his own house. Mister Nice-Bit-of-Ham had lived there.

Danny smiled.

He remembered why he'd given him that name.

CHAPTER SIX

"A sliced pan and two pints of milk," said Billy Dunne to Kay, the girl behind the counter.

Danny was thirteen. He watched Kay taking Billy Dunne's bread off the bread tray. She was lovely. Danny always went to the shop for his mother, just to see Kay. Billy Dunne always went to the shop for his mother too. But Billy Dunne was forty.

"Oh yes," said Billy Dunne. "I nearly forgot. And a nice bit of ham.

And that was it. Danny gave him the name and by the end of the day Billy Dunne was Mister Nice-Bit-of-Ham. Just like that. And for the rest of his life he was Mister Nice-Bit-of-Ham. Even Danny's mother and father called him Mister Nice-Bit-of-Ham. Even Father Clarke, the parish priest, ended up calling him Mister Nice-Bit-of-Ham.

Billy Dunne was forty and still living at home with his mother.

"She should throw him out," Danny's father often said. "He should get himself a girl."

"Who'd have him?" His mother always said.

But then Billy Dunne's mother died and before she was dead a week Billy Dunne did have a girl. And she moved into the house with Billy Dunne.

"A girl?" said Danny's mother. "She's sixty if she's a day."

Danny and Jimmy sat on Billy Dunne's wall. They were waiting for Billy Dunne. They wanted to see his girl. Billy Dunne always came home from work at the same time. Ten-to-six. He got off the same bus every day.

"Ma says she's sixty," said Danny.

"Da says she's no more than fifty-five," said Jimmy.

"That's still years older than Billy," said Danny.

"Fifteen," said Jimmy.

"Maybe twenty," said Danny.

Kay from the shop was only four years older than Danny. But Danny knew – he hadn't a hope. She was going with Ken Byrne. Ken Byrne was twenty and he had a motor bike. What was Billy Dunne's secret? He didn't even have a push bike.

"Here they come," said Jimmy.

Billy Dunne got off the bus. His girl got off after him.

"They got it wrong," said Jimmy.

"Yes," said Danny.

She wasn't old at all. At least, she was no older than Billy Dunne. She was no girl but she wasn't a granny either. She was a woman. A real woman. A real, good-looking woman. And she was holding Billy Dunne's hand. The two of them were smiling as they walked up the road.

Danny and Jimmy waited.

She had lipstick. She had high heels. She had a handbag with a gold strap. She smiled at Danny and Jimmy.

"Hello, Mister Nice-Bit-of-Ham," said Jimmy.

"Hello, Missis Nice-Bit-of-Ham," said Danny.

They jumped off the wall and ran.

They heard Billy Dunne.

"Come back here!"

They heard Billy Dunne's girl.

"Don't mind them, William," she shouted. "They're only LITTLE boys. God love them!"

Danny and Jimmy ran, and laughed. They heard Billy Dunne's girl again.

"Little BOYS! Running away! They're not worth chasing!"

CHAPTER SEVEN

Danny was still at the estate agent's window.

He was still looking at Billy Dunne's house. It was a sad-looking place. It hadn't been painted in all those years. It looked grey and very small. It seemed to be sinking into the ground. And still, it was going for £115,000.

Billy Dunne was dead. He died two days after he retired. But he didn't die because he had nothing left to live for. He was hit by a bus. He was hit by the ten-to-six bus. If he hadn't retired he'd have been on the bus instead of under it. That was what Danny had said when his mother told him.

"That's a terrible thing to say," said his mother. Just before she started laughing.

Danny didn't know what had happened to Billy Dunne's girl. She had moved out of the house and, after that, there was no more news of her.

For years, between the ages of thirteen and seventeen, Billy Dunne's girl had made Danny's life a misery. Just because he had called her Missis Nice-Bit-of-Ham. Every day after that, for the next four years, she got back at him. She never left him alone. She smiled at him. She winked. She even pinched his bum once, when they were coming out of Mass.

She just never left him alone. Danny loved Kay from the shop, even if she was going with Ken Byrne and his motor bike. He adored her. Going to the shop to look at her was the best part of every day. But when Danny lay on his bed in the dark, he could think only of Billy Dunne's girl. He didn't want to think only of Billy Dunne's girl. He didn't want to. He didn't like her. He hated her. But every time he closed his eyes she was there instead of Kay.

Now, twenty-five years later – more – Danny smiled. But at the time it hadn't been funny. He had stopped walking past Billy Dunne's house. He had stopped going to the shop for his mother. He even stopped sitting on the wall at the end of the road. The last time he went to sit on the wall, to look at the world going by, Billy Dunne's girl was there already, sitting on the wall, waiting for him. She waved at him.

He ran all the way home. He didn't come out for days. By the time he went to the shop again, Kay wasn't working there anymore. Billy Dunne's girl was.

She smiled at him when he came in the door.

"Can I help you?" she said.

"No!" Danny shouted.

He ran out of the shop.

He was worried that Jimmy would find out about Billy Dunne's girl.

And Jimmy *did* find out.

Danny would never forget it.

Jimmy and two of his pals, Ben Daly and Ringo Moon, grabbed Danny. They tied him up with a rope. They tied his feet together and they tied his hands behind his back. They pushed a hankie into Danny's mouth.

Danny knew what they were going to do.

They picked him up and carried him. Danny knew where they were going.

They carried him to Billy Dunne's house. In the gate, up the path. They left him on the step, right in front of the front door. Then they rang the bell.

Jimmy whispered into Danny's ear.

"Bye, bye, Danny," he said. "Tell her I was asking for her."

Then he ran away, after Ben and Ringo. Danny could hear them laughing.

He waited. The ropes were too tight. He couldn't move. He waited for the door to open. But nothing happened. No one came to the door. There was no one at home. But Danny still couldn't move. He was stuck.

He was still there five hours later when Billy Dunne and Billy Dunne's girl came home from work. He was asleep when they found him on the step.

He woke up when Billy Dunne was taking the hankie out of his mouth.

The first thing he heard was Billy Dunne's girl.

"Ah look, isn't he sweet?"

Danny would never, ever forget it.

They brought him into the house and he had his tea with them. Billy Dunne did the cooking. They only had two chops but Billy Dunne cut them so there was meat on the three plates.

"That's a lovely chop, William," said Billy Dunne's girl.

"Thank you, Bunny Rabbit," said Billy Dunne.

And Billy Dunne's chips were the best Danny had ever tasted.

"Who tied you up?" Billy Dunne's girl asked Danny.

"My brother," said Danny.

"Does he do it often?" she asked.

"No," said Danny.

He liked them but he couldn't wait to get out of the house. Billy Dunne ran after him when he was leaving.

"Hang on," he said. "You forgot your rope."

He handed the rope to Danny.

"Thanks," said Danny.

Danny looked at the house in the estate agent's window again. It hadn't been a sad house back then. Billy Dunne had been happy. Danny never told anyone that Billy Dunne had called his girlfriend "Bunny Rabbit".

Danny turned away from the window.

It was time to go. He was going to be ten minutes late. That was just right.

It was time to meet Jimmy.

CHAPTER EIGHT

Danny pushed the door and walked into Todd's. He walked into the dark bar. He looked around. No Jimmy. There was no one who looked like Jimmy. In fact, there was no one at all. The place was empty.

"The bastard," said Danny.

"Are you talking to me?" said a voice.

Danny still couldn't see anyone.

"No," said Danny. "Sorry, I was talking to myself."

Then he saw a head. Then the rest of the body came up from behind the counter. It was a barman. Danny saw now. It was the same barman who had served Danny and Jimmy the first time all those years ago. He looked older and fatter. But, mind you, so did Danny.

"I was looking for someone," said Danny.

"Anyone I know?" said the barman.

"My brother."

"I don't think I know him," said the barman. "There was a lad with red hair in a pony-tail in a minute ago. Is that him?"

"No," said Danny. "I don't think so."

"You don't think so?" said the barman. "Do you not know what your brother looks like?"

What colour *was* Jimmy's hair? Danny asked himself. Brown. Maybe black. Dark. But definitely not red. And what about the pony-tail? Danny didn't think that Jimmy would have a pony-tail but he didn't really know. He'd have to wait and see.

"I haven't seen him in a while," said Danny.

He walked over to the bar.

"A while?" said the barman. "His hair grows fast, does it?"

Danny was getting tired of the barman.

"A pint of Guinness, please, and mind your own business."

The barman looked at Danny.

"What age are you?" he said.

"You remember me," said Danny.

"Yes," said the barman. "I always remember a face."

He smiled.

"Are you over eighteen?" he said.

"My kids are over eighteen," said Danny.

"God love you," said the barman. "What about me? My grand-kids are over eighteen"

"You're looking well," said Danny.

"I know," said the barman. "I was always a good-looking man."

"It's quiet tonight," said Danny as he watched the barman pulling his pint.

"It's quiet every night," said the barman.

"How come?" said Danny.

"You don't live here anymore, do you?" said the barman.

"No," said Danny.

"There's your answer," said the barman. "All the old crowd have died or moved away. It's all yuppies now. And they wouldn't come into a place like this. It's nobody's local anymore."

Danny felt sorry for the barman but he couldn't think of anything to say to him.

"How's your mother?" said the barman.

"She's fine," said Danny. "I didn't know you knew her."

"I don't," said the barman. "I knew your da."

He put the pint in front of Danny.

"He told me about you and your brother," said the barman.

He pointed at the pint.

"That will be twenty-three pence," he said.

"What?" said Danny.

"Twenty-three pence," said the barman. "That was the price of the pint the first time you came in here. So give me twenty-three pence. For old time's sake."

"Thanks very much," said Danny.

He heard the door behind him opening.

CHAPTER NINE

Danny heard the door. He felt the cold wind from outside on his neck. He heard the door closing. He turned.

"Hello, Jimmy," he said.

"Look at you," said Jimmy.

He stood at the door.

"My little brother," he said.

He didn't move.

"You're looking well," said Danny.

It was true. The years had been good to Jimmy. He had more hair than Danny, and less fat. His suit had cost a lot of money.

And how did Danny feel about this man, his handsome, well-off brother standing in front of him? Good. Danny felt good. He felt very good. He was glad to see Jimmy. His smile was big and real. He wanted to laugh. It was the same old Jimmy in front of him.

He jumped off his stool and walked over to Jimmy. He put his hand out.

"It's great to see you," he said.

And he could see it in Jimmy's face. Jimmy was glad to see him too.

They shook hands and then they hugged, and Danny wanted to cry. He felt like he'd been away for years, but now he had come home.

"Is Missis Nice-Bit-of-Ham dead?" said Danny when they stopped hugging.

"Not at all," said Jimmy. "She went off with a nice bit of turkey."

It was the same old Jimmy.

"Will you have a pint?" said Danny.

"Of course I will," said Jimmy.

"Do you still drink Guinness?" said Danny.

"When I am at home," said Jimmy.

"What do you drink over there?" said Danny.

"Anything I can get my hands on," said Jimmy.

Danny ordered the pint from the barman. The barman said nothing. He kept well away from them, down at the far end of the bar.

"That's not true, by the way," said Jimmy.

"What's not true?" said Danny.

"What I said about drinking anything," said Jimmy. "I hardly drink at all."

"Neither do I," said Danny. "Just now and again. A few pints."

"How did you get so fat then?" said Jimmy.

Danny didn't let himself get angry or upset. It was the same old Jimmy.

"Food," he said.

"Too much food," said Jimmy.

"No," said Danny. "Enough food, too often. That's all. And anyway, I felt plenty of fat when I was hugging you there."

"That's the job of a good suit," said Jimmy.

He rubbed his jacket.

"It hides what you don't want the world to see," said Jimmy. "Do you want to know how much I paid for it?"

"No," said Danny.

"More than you make in a month," said Jimmy.

Again, Danny didn't let himself get angry or upset. It was the same old Jimmy alright. Still a spoofer, still a big mouth.

CHAPTER TEN

Danny was five.

He was standing between his Uncle Jim's knees, in the kitchen. He liked his Uncle Jim. He always had sweets in his pockets when he came to the house. He always let Danny and Jimmy look for them. And he always made sure that they found the same amount of sweets each.

"Were you good in school this week, Dan-Dan?" said Uncle Jim.

It was Sunday, a day Uncle Jim always came to the house.

"Yes," said Danny.

"What did you learn?" said Uncle Jim.

"I forget," said Danny.

"How far can you count?" said Uncle Jim.

"Real far," said Danny. "One, two, three, four …"

Suddenly, Jimmy was there. And, suddenly, Jimmy was standing between his Uncle's knees and Danny was on the floor.

"I can count forever," said Jimmy. "Do you want to hear me?"

"Fire away," said Uncle Jim.

"One, two, three, four, five, six, seven, eight …"

Later, in bed, Jimmy pushed Danny.

"I got my name from Uncle Jim," he said. "You got your name from no one."

"Then how come you're Jimmy, not Jim?" said Danny.

"I'll be called Jim when I'm a man," said Jimmy. "You're a thick-looking eejit."

"I got my name from a saint," said Danny.

"Saint Danny?" said Jimmy. " I never heard of him."

"Saint Daniel," said Danny. "He took a spike out of a lion's paw."

"And then the lion ate him because he was a thick-looking eejit like you," said Jimmy.

Danny cried but no one downstairs heard him.

"Cry baby, cry baby," said Jimmy. "People called Jim never cry. People called Danny always cry."

CHAPTER ELEVEN

The barman put a new pint on the counter.

"One nice pint," he said.

Danny paid him. He handed the pint to Jimmy and they walked over to the corner they had hidden in the first time they had been in here. The exact same table, the same chairs. The same beer mats. The paint was new, though. And there was a picture that hadn't been there before. It was a photograph of the city taken from a crane or helicopter. "Dublin – City of Culture."

They sat down.

Jimmy lifted his pint.

"Cheers," he said.

"Cheers," said Danny.

"How long is it since we were here?" Jimmy asked.

"Twenty years," said Danny. "More."

"A lot more," said Jimmy. "Nearly thirty. You remember that night, do you?"

"I do, indeed," said Danny.

They smiled, and laughed.

"We were wild men," said Jimmy.

"That's right," said Danny.

They said nothing for a while. Danny lifted his glass again, just to be doing something.

"Well, cheers anyway," he said.

"Yes," said Jimmy. "Cheers."

"So, Jimmy," said Danny.

"Jim," said Jimmy.

"What?" said Danny.

"Jim," said Jimmy. "My name's Jim."

Danny was being mean. He knew it. But he couldn't help it.

"Since when?" he said.

"Since a long time before I left," said Jimmy. "So, don't start."

"Okay," said Danny. "Jim."

"Dan," said Jimmy.

"My name's Danny," said Danny.

"Fine," said Jimmy. "I was just checking."

It was hard to believe. All this time away from each other and it was like they had never been apart. They were already fighting, already biting at each other. And yet, at the same time, Danny was still glad to be with Jimmy. It was strange. People said that you could love and hate the same person. And Danny knew that it was true.

"So," said Danny. "What brings you home?"

"I often come home," said Jimmy. "Once a year. More sometimes."

Danny knew this. His mother always told him when Jimmy was coming home and Danny always stayed away until Jimmy was gone back.

Jimmy spoke now.

"What you want to know is, why did I phone *you*?"

"Yes," said Danny. "That's right."

"I meant to before," said Jimmy. "Every time I came home. I was going to phone you. I was going to ask you to come over to London with your wife and kids. For a holiday. I was always going to. But then I thought, why should I? He never phones me. So why should I phone him."

Jimmy took a drink and spoke again. "And I bet you started the exact same thing. Why should I? I didn't start it. Am I right?"

Danny nodded.

"It's gas, isn't it?" said Jimmy. "Big boys like us behaving like that and I bet you something else."

He looked at Danny.

Danny didn't want to talk. He didn't

trust his voice.

He was afraid he'd cry. *Cry baby. Cry baby. People called Danny always cry.* So he only spoke one word.

"What?"

"I bet you give out to your kids if *they* behave like we did. Am I right?"

Danny nodded.

"Me too," said Jimmy.

Danny didn't know how many kids Jimmy had. His mother had told him but he had never listened.

Jimmy took another drink and spoke.

"So here I am."

He put his hand out.

"It's good to see you, Danny," he said. "Really. And if you start crying I'll walk out of here and you will never see me again."

They laughed, and Danny let his tears flow.

"Are you crying?" said Jimmy.

"No," said Danny. "Not really."

But he was.

"She wasn't a bad-looking woman," said Jimmy. "Sure she wasn't?"

"Who?" said Danny.

"Missus Nice-Bit-of-Ham."

Danny thought about this.

"I didn't think so at the time," he said. "But now I'd think she was lovely."

Jimmy nodded.

"Is that a good thing or a bad thing about getting old?" he asked.

"What?" said Danny.

"You know," said Jimmy. "Liking women of all ages, as well as the young ones."

"It fills the day," said Danny.

"You're right there," said Jimmy. "Anyway, no young one would look at us now. Do you know something?"

"What?"

"I've never told anyone else this."

"I won't tell anyone," said Danny.

"You'd better not," said Jimmy.

"Go on," said Danny.

"I'm after falling in love with my mother-in-law."

Danny laughed.

"Laugh away," said Jimmy. "But it's true."

Danny laughed again. He remembered Jimmy's mother-in-law. He remembered her well. He tried not to think of her daughter, Jimmy's wife. It had all been a long time ago. It didn't matter anymore.

He laughed.

"I couldn't help it," said Jimmy. "She's seventy-seven and I think she's a ride."

Danny lifted his pint.

"Women," he said.

"Now you're talking," said Jimmy.

And he lifted his pint.

"Women."

CHAPTER TWELVE

Danny and Jimmy, aged fourteen and fifteen, lay in the sand and watched the girls go by. They were in Skerries, for the last two weeks in July. Their father was off playing pitch and putt. Their mother was down the beach with their sister, well away from Jimmy and Danny.

"I like mine but I don't like yours."

"I don't like yours."

"The tall one?"

"Yes."

"She's yours, you sap."

"She's not. I saw the other one first."

"Prove it."

"I can't."

"She's mine, so."

"That's not fair."

"Tough."

The girl they were fighting about was, in fact nearly a woman. She was years older than them. She never even looked at them as she walked past.

"Maybe she has a sister."

"I don't want her sister."

"She might be nice."

"I don't want her bloody sister."

All day they lay there on the sand. Their backs got redder and redder. They knew they were being burnt but they couldn't take their eyes off the girls. And their mothers. And their sisters and aunts and grannys. They were all well worth the sunburn, and the pain, and the blisters.

A big gang of girls came down from the road onto the beach.

"Look," said Jimmy.

Danny counted them. There were

seven girls, all walking towards him. They all looked the same age as Danny.

"Look at them," said Jimmy.

"I am," said Danny.

They were all different. There was a tall one. There was a very small one. There was a fat one, but not too fat. A thin one. Three tanned ones. Four red ones. Three with fair hair. One with red hair. Two with black hair. One with a nice nose. Three with big ears. Two of them were really beautiful. Three of them weren't beautiful at all.

But Danny loved them all. He wanted to stand up and walk over to them. He wanted to smile and walk right into the middle of them. He wanted to talk to them. He wanted to sit with them for the rest of the day. He wanted to make them laugh.

He wanted one of them to take his hand and hold it. He wanted to walk along the beach with her at the end of the day.

He didn't mind which one, any of them. He just wanted to walk along the beach. He wanted to feel her hand in his. It was so easy. He just had to stand up and go over to them.

But he couldn't. He knew he couldn't. He could never go over there. He would never be able to talk. He knew it. It made him hate himself and it made him hate the girls. Ugly, cruel words came into his head. He wanted to shout them at the girls.

"Come on," said Jimmy.

Jimmy stood up and walked over to the girls. Just like that. He left Danny lying there. On the sand. By himself. He watched Jimmy go over to the girls. He watched Jimmy sitting down. Jimmy turned around and waved at him. He was trying to get Danny to follow him.

Danny hid behind the sand-grass.

He heard one of the girls laughing. Jimmy had made her laugh.

"Stand up," Danny said to himself. "Stand up. It's easy. Go on. Now is your chance. Just follow Jimmy."

But he couldn't.

He stayed where he was. When he looked again Jimmy and the girls were gone.

CHAPTER THIRTEEN

Back in the pub, Danny remembered the day at the beach in Skerries.

Jimmy had gone up to the bar to get his round.

It was a day that Danny often remembered. He had told lots of people about it. He had told his wife about it, more than once. The first time he had told her he had cried. *People called Danny always cry.* He had told his mother. He had told so many friends down the years, more than he could ever count. People in work, men in a pub, women he knew before he met his wife. He'd told them all.

Years after it had happened. He had told them about Jimmy standing up and leaving him alone. Jimmy was always the bad guy. Danny was always the little brother left behind. The little boy left all alone.

He knew now. He had been lying to them all. He had told the same story so often, for so long, he had believed it. He had never told them about the fun they had that day. He never told them how Jimmy had told him to follow him, or how Jimmy had waved at him to come over. He never told them that he had been just too shy to follow Jimmy.

All these years Jimmy had been the bad guy. Danny had made it up. Just because Jimmy had been brave enough to stand up and say "Hello" to the girls and Danny had been too shy.

Danny watched Jimmy as he came back from the bar with the new pints. He wondered how many of his other memories were made-up and how many were real.

Jimmy sat down.

"What about *your* mother-in-law?" he said. "What's she like?"

"Dead," said Danny.

"Oops," said Jimmy.

He lifted his new pint.

"Cheers again," he said.

Danny could hardly look at Jimmy now. He felt so bad. He wanted to say something but he didn't know how to start.

Then Jimmy saved him.

"Do you remember the time we became blood brothers?" said Jimmy.

"Yes," said Danny.

"It was stupid really," said Jimmy. "I mean, we were brothers already."

"Yes," said Danny. "That was what I said at the time."

Danny remembered it, and he knew he wasn't making it up. He was remembering something that had really happened.

"You still grabbed my hand and cut my finger," he told Jimmy.

"It was just a bit of crack," said Jimmy.

"And I ended up in hospital," said Danny.

He looked at his finger. It was the middle one on his right hand. He saw the thin scar across the top of the finger. He lifted his hand and his finger and turned it so that Jimmy could see the scar.

"Look," he said.

"What?" said Jimmy.

"The scar," said Danny.

"What scar?" said Jimmy. "I can't see a scar."

Danny moved his hand nearer to Jimmy's face.

"Now can you?" he said.

"It's tiny," said Jimmy.

Danny felt better. Not all of his memories were made-up or unfair to Jimmy. He could see it in Jimmy's face. Jimmy remembered what he had done to

Danny that day.

"You can put your hand down now," said Jimmy. "I've seen your war wound."

Danny could tell Jimmy was angry. And that made Danny feel even better.

Jimmy stared down at the table.

CHAPTER FOURTEEN

Danny was nine, Jimmy was ten. They were in a field near their house. There would soon be new houses on it but, for now, it was still a field.

They were alone. Just Danny, Jimmy and the bread-knife.

"Hold out your hand," said Jimmy.

"No," said Danny.

"Go on," said Jimmy. "Don't be such a sissy."

"No," said Danny.

He sat on his hands.

"We have to mix our blood," said Jimmy. "It won't hurt."

"No," said Danny.

"We have to do it if we are going to be blood brothers," said Jimmy.

"We're brothers already," said Danny.

He saw Jimmy looking at his hands. He pushed them well under his bum.

Then he fell for the trick. He fell for the oldest trick in the book.

"Look!" said Jimmy.

He pointed at something above Danny's head.

"What?" said Danny.

He looked up at – nothing.

He felt Jimmy's fingers around his wrist. Before he could stop him, Jimmy pulled Danny's hand out from under him. He saw the blade of the bread-knife go quickly across the top of his finger.

He saw blood. He saw the shock on Jimmy's face.

"I didn't mean it."

He saw the blood running down his finger, down his hand, down into his sleeve. He saw an ant on a blade of grass beside his knee. He saw his sleeve changing colour. He saw a cloud that looked like a map of Ireland.

"Danny!"

He felt his head hit the ground. He saw the grass, every blade of grass in the world. He felt the pain. All the pain in the world was in the tip of his finger.

"Danny!"

He felt his lids closing over his eyes.

He saw nothing else.

He felt nothing else.

CHAPTER FIFTEEN

Back in the pub, Jimmy stared at the table. He was remembering the same day.

He was ten. Danny was nine.

Jimmy had already cut his own finger with the bread-knife. There was a drop of blood sitting on the tip of the middle finger of the left hand. It was waiting to join Danny's blood.

But Danny had changed his mind.

"Go on," said Jimmy. "Don't be such a sissy."

"No," said Danny.

Danny sat on his hands.

"Go on," said Jimmy. "It won't hurt. It didn't hurt me. Look."

Jimmy held up his cut finger.

"No," said Danny.

Then Jimmy played a trick on Danny. It was the same old trick he had played on Danny millions of times before. Danny fell for it every time. He pointed above Danny's head.

"Look!"

"What?" said Danny.

He looked up at the sky.

Jimmy grabbed Danny's wrist and pulled his hand. Danny tried to pull his hand back, but then he stopped. Jimmy looked at him.

"Okay?" he said.

"Okay," said Danny.

He stuck out his middle finger. Jimmy put the blade of the bread-knife to the finger's tip.

Then Danny changed his mind again. He chickened out. He tried to pull his hand out of Jimmy's grip. Jimmy wouldn't let go. Danny pulled again and his finger slid across the blade.

Jimmy watched.

For what seemed like hours nothing happened. Then, he saw the blood. And he felt his own blood draining from his face. He wanted to get sick.

The blood rushed from Danny's finger. Jimmy didn't know what to do.

"I didn't mean it," he said.

It was all he could think of.

Danny's whole hand was now red. Jimmy saw the blood rushing into Danny's shirt sleeve. He saw it falling onto the grass.

He saw Danny's eyes closing.

"Danny!"

Danny fell back. His head hit the grass. He had fainted.

"Danny!"

Jimmy got up. His legs were weak. He thought he was going to fall. But he didn't. He looked down at Danny.

Danny's face was very white. He looked dead. There was no life at all in his face.

Jimmy dropped the bread-knife onto the ground. He rubbed Danny's cheeks. They were cold.

"Danny!"

Jimmy was crying now. He had never been so scared in his life. He had killed his brother. Danny was dead. He didn't know what he was going to do.

"Danny. Wake up!"

He picked up Danny. Danny was heavy, nearly the same size as Jimmy. But Jimmy picked him up easily.

He carried Danny all the way home. He saw the blood dropping onto the ground, first the grass, then onto the path. But he didn't stop.

Danny started to moan. It was the best sound Jimmy had ever heard. Danny was alive. But Jimmy kept going.

Danny opened his eyes.

"Sorry, Danny," said Jimmy. "Can you hear me?"

"Yes," said Danny.

But he closed his eyes again.

Jimmy carried him all the way home.

He rang the bell and waited for his mother or father to come to the door.

CHAPTER SIXTEEN

Back in the pub, Danny was still looking at the old scar at the tip of his finger.

Jimmy looked at him.

There was sweat on his forehead. He felt very hot. It was like he had just run all the way from the field to the house, all over again, with Danny in his arms. Now, years later – years and years later – he could feel his heart pumping, as if it had all happened a minute ago. He could feel the ground under his running feet. He could feel Danny's body in his arms.

Danny looked up and saw Jimmy looking back at him.

"What's wrong?" said Danny.

Jimmy looked sick.

"Nothing," said Jimmy.

He wiped his forehead with his hand.

"It would never have happened if you hadn't pulled your hand back," he said.

"You were the one with the knife," said Danny.

"You were the one who told Ma and Da that I stabbed you," said Jimmy.

Jimmy remembered it. On the way to Jervis Street Hospital. Danny was in the back of the car with their mother, and Jimmy was in the front with their father.

Danny's hand was wrapped in a tea towel. He was awake and crying.

"He stabbed me, Ma!"

Jimmy remembered it. His father's hand was back on the steering wheel before Jimmy felt the pain or heard the smack. His father had just hit him with the back of his hand.

Jimmy tasted blood in his mouth.

Now, back in the pub, Danny spoke.

"I never told them you stabbed me," he said.

"You did," said Jimmy.

"I didn't."

"You did!"

The scars on Jimmy's neck had gone very white and ugly. And the long scar high up on Jimmy's forehead wasn't hidden by his hair anymore.

Danny looked away.

"There's no need to shout," he said.

It was the same old Jimmy. He was trying to blame Danny for something he'd done himself. Making it up when it suited him. Making Danny play the part.

Danny remembered that trip to the hospital. He remembered it well. He had never told his mother and father that Jimmy had stabbed him. He had never said anything like that.

"Jimmy had the knife, Ma."

That was what he had said.

"Jimmy had the knife, Ma."

That was all.

"What knife?" said his mother.

"The bread-knife," said Danny.

"*My* bread-knife?" said his mother.

She spoke to Jimmy.

"You nearly killed your own brother with *my* bread-knife."

And then she shouted.

"How dare you!"

And their father hit Jimmy.

And now, back in the pub, Jimmy wanted to hit Danny because Danny had started laughing.

"What's so funny?" he said.

"What happened to the bread-knife?"

"What bread-knife?" said Jimmy.

"The one you stabbed me with," said Danny.

And Jimmy leaned over the table and hit Danny in the chest.

"I didn't bloody stab you!"

There was no air in Danny's lungs. For

a few long seconds he couldn't breathe. He held onto the table. He saw the barman looking over at them. He saw Jimmy staring at him, ready to hit him again.

Jimmy was very angry and, now that he could breathe again, Danny felt good about it. This was the real Jimmy. This was the creep who had made Danny's life a misery. This was why he had had nothing to do with him all these years. And he'd been right. He was nothing but a bully. And Danny wasn't going to hit him back. That was what Jimmy wanted him to do.

It was Jimmy who spoke first.

"You always were the mammy's boy," he said.

"Grow up," said Danny.

"You're the one who should grow up," said Jimmy. "You never could stand up for yourself. Someone else was always to blame. You were always running to Ma. And you haven't changed a bit."

"Get lost."

"I'll get lost when I'm ready to," said Jimmy. "I've been living over there …"

Jimmy pointed at the pub door but Danny knew that he meant London. Jimmy's voice was shaking.

"I've been living over there for the last twenty years because of you. Do you think I wanted to leave?"

"I didn't make you leave," said Danny.

"You did!" said Jimmy. "One of us had to go and it was never going to be you. You hadn't the guts. If I hadn't gone I would have killed you or you would have killed me. I was no angel, I know that. But at least I didn't pretend I was. Like you."

"She was my girlfriend!" said Danny.

"Only for as long as she wanted to be," said Jimmy.

"And you got off with her," said Danny.

"I didn't," said Jimmy. "She got off with *me*. She wanted *me*. Not you. It was simple. But you couldn't see it."

Jimmy took a drink. He could hold the glass now without it shaking.

"She's well, by the way," said Jimmy.

"I don't care how she is," said Danny.

She was Barbara Kelly. She'd been Danny's girlfriend all those years ago. And now, she was Jimmy's wife.

"You didn't care about her back then either," said Jimmy.

Danny said nothing. Jimmy was right but Danny was trying to remember it a different way. He tried to remember love. He tried to remember walking hand in hand with Barbara. He tried to remember the colour of her eyes, or her hair. But it didn't work. All he could remember was the anger and the shock. And the blood.

"You just pretended you cared," said Jimmy. "I loved her and I still love her but you didn't give a damn about her. You just wanted her, so I couldn't have her. You were always like that."

Danny stood up.

"Goodbye, Jimmy."

"My name's Jim," said Jimmy. "Sit down, I have something to tell you."

CHAPTER SEVENTEEN

Danny could remember the shock.

He walked into the kitchen and saw Jimmy. Then he saw Barbara. They were three feet apart. They were as far apart as they could be in a small kitchen. And they were both looking at Danny.

Danny knew. They had been kissing just before he'd walked into the kitchen. They had jumped away from each other. And he knew another thing. He wasn't shocked at all. He had expected to see Jimmy and Barbara when he walked in. That was *why* he had walked in. He didn't know at the time, but now he did. He had wanted to catch them.

And he had.

There they were.

Trapped. Snared. Guilty. It was written across their faces. Their red, red faces.

"Hi, Danny," said Barbara.

Blue. Danny remembered now. Her eyes were blue. Twenty years ago. More. Deep, deep blue. He remembered staring at Barbara, then at Jimmy for a second. Then he turned around and walked out of the kitchen.

He heard Jimmy behind him.

"Danny!"

He kept walking.

His feelings were mixed. In a way, he was glad. He had been going with Barbara, and now he wasn't, and that was fine. And she was to blame. He had caught her with Jimmy, and he was glad about that too.

Danny was good, Jimmy was bad. Danny was nice, Jimmy wasn't. Walking into the kitchen had proved that. Danny had caught his brother messing with his girlfriend. Everybody would be on Danny's side.

But he was angry too. They had made a fool of him. Everyone would know about it. His own brother had robbed his girl. They would laugh at him. They would point at him. There he is, Danny the sap. So he was angry. He was angry and glad and guilty.

And he was angry when Jimmy grabbed his arm. They were in the hall. Danny was on his way to the front door.

"Hang on, Danny," said Jimmy.

He pulled Danny's arm. Danny saw Barbara behind Jimmy. She looked worried.

Danny pulled his arm away.

"Get your hands off me," he said.

Jimmy lifted his open hands into the air, as if he was being arrested.

"Okay, okay," he said. "Just wait, will you."

Jimmy now stood between Danny and the door.

Danny pushed him. He tried to push him out of the way. But the hall was very narrow. There wasn't much room.

Danny pushed him again.

"Get out of my way!" he shouted.

Their mother and father and their sisters, Una and Mary, were all in bed. It was well past midnight.

"Get out of my way!" Danny shouted again.

Jimmy tried to stop Danny again. Danny pushed his chest. Jimmy grabbed his arms and the two of them fell onto the floor. Danny fell on top of Jimmy.

Barbara screamed.

Jimmy was angry now too. They had both been drinking. They'd been drinking all night.

Jimmy thumped Danny. Danny lifted

his knee between Jimmy's legs. Jimmy grunted, and rolled off Danny. Danny began to stand up but Jimmy pulled him back. Jimmy started to hit Danny, hard. He thumped his chest, his arms, his face. Danny grabbed Jimmy's hair.

Over all their noise Danny could hear Barbara's screams.

"Stop! Stop it!"

They both got to their feet. They stared at each other. There was blood coming from Jimmy's nose and Danny could feel blood on his lip.

Just there, just then, Danny and Jimmy hated each other.

They heard their parents' bedroom door opening.

"What's going on down there?"

It was their father.

"Boys?"

And their mother.

Jimmy ran at Danny. He was bigger than Danny. Not much bigger but big enough to knock Danny back. Danny grabbed Jimmy's shirt as he fell.

He fell. They both fell – back, back, back – through the front door. Through the glass of the front door. Right through the glass. Danny felt it. He heard it caving in as his head and shoulders went through the glass.

There was nothing behind him now. He fell through the air. He knew that he was in trouble. He knew that there was going to be pain. He knew that he was going to be hurt and that Jimmy was going to be hurt. He knew that they were going to be badly hurt.

He heard the screams.

He heard glass breaking, smashing. He heard more screams.

His back hit the step outside, and the back of his head hit the corner of the step.

More screams.

"Jimmy!"

It was Barbara. She was shouting for Jimmy.

It was Jimmy's fault. He had pushed Danny through the glass. He had started the fight. He had tried to take Danny's girl.

Danny closed his eyes.

CHAPTER EIGHTEEN

"Sit down," said Jimmy. "I have something to tell you."

There was something about the way Jimmy said it. Danny quickly sat back down.

He looked at Jimmy.

Jimmy spoke quietly.

"I'm dying," he said.

Suddenly, Danny felt very heavy. His body heard the news before his brain did. It took a long time for Jimmy's words to have any meaning.

It took even longer for Danny to speak. His mouth was open a long time before anything came out.

"How?" he said.

"The usual," said Jimmy.

It was a real Jimmy answer. Danny almost smiled.

"Cancer?" he asked.

"Yes," said Jimmy.

"Jesus," said Danny.

"And his mother," said Jimmy.

"How long have you got?" Danny asked.

"Months," said Jimmy. "A year at most."

"Jesus, Jimmy," said Danny. "I'm sorry."

"Jesus, Danny, so am I," said Jimmy. "But do me a favour before I die."

"What?"

"Call me Jim."

"Right. Right, okay. Sorry. Jim."

"No problem," said Jimmy.

They said nothing for a while. Then Jimmy spoke.

"So."

And that was all for another while. It was plenty. It was a word full of meaning. It was a word full of the forty years that the two men had lived together and apart. It was a word full of love, anger, fun, pain. It was a word that offered a new start.

"Yes," said Danny after a few long seconds. "So."

"So here we are," said Jimmy.

"Yes," said Danny.

"It's good to see you, Danny," said Jimmy. "And if you start crying I'll murder you."

They had two more pints, and two more, and two more after that. They talked and talked. They filled in all the missing years. Danny told Jimmy about his kids, his job, his house, his wife. Jimmy told Danny about his job, his part of London, his kids, Barbara and his mother-in-law. They talked about their father, and how they missed him. They talked about their mother, and their worries about her. They talked about their sisters and their husbands, how they both liked one husband and couldn't stand the other one. They talked about music and films. They talked about football. They talked about everything. They made up for the lost time and the time that was running out. They talked about everything except death.

Closing time came and went. The lights of the bar went on and off. They got two six-packs from the barman. He wouldn't take money from them.

"I knew your da," he said. "He'd be a happy man tonight."

They went outside. It was raining but they didn't have to wait long for a taxi. They went back to Danny's house and Jimmy met Karen, Danny's wife, for the first time. They shook hands and Jimmy kissed her cheek.

Danny smiled. He was proud of his wife. He was proud of his brother.

Karen went up to bed and left them alone in the kitchen.

"She's nice," said Jimmy.

"Better looking than Barbara," said Danny.

"Ah now," said Jimmy. "Neck and neck, I'd say. We'll all go somewhere together, will we? For the holidays."

"Yes," said Danny.

"It'll be good," said Jimmy.

"Yes," said Danny.

"A few weeks in the summer."

"Yes."

"If I make it that far," said Jimmy.

Danny said nothing. He looked at Jimmy. Now, in the kitchen, he loved him as much as he loved his children. He wanted to hug him. He wanted to hug him for the rest of their lives. He wanted to take Jimmy's pain and make him live forever.

"I'm sorry, Jimmy," he said.

"Jim," said Jimmy.

"Jim," said Danny. "For everything."

That was all he could say. His eyes filled with tears. He let them flow onto his cheeks. He tried to speak again.

"I'm sorry."

"Danny," said Jimmy.

Danny wiped his eyes.

"What?"

"I have something else to tell you."

"What?" said Danny.

"The cancer," said Jimmy.

"What about it?" said Danny.

"I don't have it," said Jimmy.

Danny didn't understand.

"I'm fine," said Jimmy. "There's nothing wrong with me."

He wasn't smiling. He wasn't joking.

Danny wasn't angry. But he still didn't understand.

"Why did you tell me you had it?" he asked.

"It was the only thing I could think of," said Jimmy. "If I hadn't said it, you'd have walked out of the pub. We would never have seen each other again."

Danny put both his hands on the kitchen table.

"Jesus," he said.

Jimmy said nothing.

"So you're not dying?" said Danny.

"No," said Jimmy. "No quicker than you, anyway."

Danny looked at the table, then at the window, then at the roof. Then at Jimmy.

"Well, that's good news," he said.

"Yes," said Jimmy. "I did such a good job I was beginning to think I *did* have cancer."

They said nothing for a while. Then Danny spoke.

"Why *did* you phone me?"

"I told you," said Jimmy. "I'd been meaning to do it for years. Then there was this ad on the telly."

"What?"

"I was watching the telly with Barbara

a few months ago," said Jimmy. "And the ad came on. You know the one. *Dogs are for life, not just for Christmas.* Do you know it?"

"Yes," said Danny.

"Well," said Jimmy. "When it was over Barbara said, 'So are brothers.' *She* made me do it. She kept at me. For months. So here I am."

"So I'm a dog, am I?" said Danny.

"Yes," said Jimmy. "And so am I."

"Woof," said Danny.

"Woof," said Jimmy.

"Woof, woof."

"Woof, woof, woof."

Danny laughed.

And Jimmy laughed

They laughed together and for a long time.

Vocabulary

PAGE 3
a pint
Maßangabe (hier:) ein grosses Bier

PAGE 5
(to) **smack** schlagen
hangover Kater

PAGE 6
fart Furz
(to) **be sore** schmerzen

PAGE 7
(to) **yell** schreien, rufen

PAGE 8
Coronation Street
English soap opera (im Fernsehen seit 1960)

PAGE 10
(to) **crawl** kriechen
Mind yourself! Pass auf dich auf!

PAGE 11
arse Arsch, Hintern
chest Oberkörper, Brustkorb

PAGE 15
(to) **curse** fluchen

PAGE 17
(to) **grab** packen, schnappen

PAGE 18
gut Bauch

PAGE 19
chipper Frittenbude

PAGE 20
(to) **puke** (er)brechen
estate agency Wohnungsmaklerbüro

PAGE 22
sliced pan in Scheiben geschnittenes Brot

PAGE 25
high heels Stöckelschuhe
(to) **chase** jagen

PAGE 26
(to) **retire** in Rente / Pension gehen

PAGE 27
(to) **wink** zwinkern
(to) **pinch** zwicken
bum Hintern
(to) **adore** anbeten

PAGE 28
(to) **wave**   winken

PAGE 29
(to) **grab**   greifen, schnappen
hankie   Taschentuch

PAGE 30
(to) **be stuck**   festsitzen
chop   Kotelett

PAGE 33
counter   Tresen

PAGE 34
lad   junger Kerl, Bursche

PAGE 36
crowd   Leute

PAGE 38
handsome   gutaussehend

PAGE 39
(to) **hug**   sich umarmen
nice bit of turkey
   (hier:) ziemlicher Fatzke

PAGE 41
spoofer   Angeber

PAGE 42
amount   Menge

PAGE 43
eejit *(Irish English for idiot)*   Idiot

PAGE 44
spike   Stachel
paw   Pfote, Tatze, Pranke

PAGE 46
mean   gemein

PAGE 47
(to) **check**   überprüfen

PAGE 48
it's gas
   es ist zum Schreien
(to) **trust**   vertrauen

PAGE 49
(to) **give out to**
   schimpfen mit

PAGE 51
I'm after falling in love   ich habe mich gerade verliebt
she's a ride   sie ist toll *(im Bett)*

PAGE 52
pitch and putt   Minigolf
sap   Depp, Trottel

PAGE 53
bloody   verflucht

blister (Haut-)Blase

PAGE 54
tanned gebräunt

PAGE 60
crack Witz, Spaß
scar Narbe

PAGE 62
sissy Memme, Waschlappen

PAGE 64
sleeve Ärmel
ant Ameise

PAGE 66
(to) **chicken out** kneifen

PAGE 67
(to) **faint** das Bewusstsein verlieren

PAGE 68
(to) **be scared** Angst haben
(to) **moan** stöhnen

PAGE 70
forehead Stirn

PAGE 71
(to) **stab** einstechen auf
(to) **wrap** umwickeln
steering wheel Lenkrad

PAGE 72
(to) **blame** beschuldigen, verantwortlich machen
(to) **suit** passen

PAGE 74
creep Widerling, fieser Typ
misery Qual
bully Rüpel, Rabauke

PAGE 75
guts Mumm, Schneid, Mut
(to) **pretend** vorgeben

PAGE 76
anger Wut
(to) **pretend** vortäuschen, vorgeben

PAGE 79
trapped gefangen *(mit einer Falle, z.B. Fuchs)*
snared gefangen *(mit einer Falle, z.B. Vogel)*
guilty schuldig

PAGE 80
(to) **prove** beweisen
(to) **mess with** sb. herummachen mit jdm.
(to) **rob** rauben, stehlen

PAGE 81
(to) **thump** (ein)schlagen

PAGE 82
(to) **grunt** grunzen

PAGE 83
(to) **cave in** einstürzen, zusammenbrechen

PAGE 85
brain Gehirn

PAGE 86
cancer Krebs

PAGE 91
ad Werbung, Spot